LOG
OFF

LOG OFF

OFF

SELF-HELP FOR THE EXTREMELY ONLINE

SAMMY NICKALLS

SPRUCE BOOKS
A Sasquatch Books Imprint

"ONCE MEN TURNED
THEIR THINKING OVER TO
MACHINES IN THE HOPE THAT
THIS WOULD SET THEM FREE.
BUT THAT ONLY PERMITTED
OTHER MEN WITH MACHINES
TO ENSLAVE THEM."

—FRANK HERBERT, *DUNE*

CONTENTS

INTRODUCTION:
LOGGING OFF IS HARD TO DO

Isn't it obnoxious when someone goes on and on about "digital detoxing"? Like, we get it, you think you're "evolved" or whatever.

Besides, I'd say that by now, most of us have grasped the concept that being on your phone too much is Bad. It's been shoved in our faces by the news with clickbait and shocking chyrons, preached to us by older generations who jump at the chance to talk about how social media wasn't around when they were growing up, and detailed in (admittedly terrifying) documentaries like *The Social Dilemma*.

So what's the problem? In a nutshell, studies show that in 2020, American teens spent an average of seven and a half hours on their phone daily—and that we should be spending less than two hours a day on screen time if we want to, ya know, *not* be miserable.

Let's be real, though: it's just not that easy! Within our screens are also our friends, our connections, our networks, and—particularly during the pandemic—our strongest link to the world at large. Like, try detoxing from *that*, buddy.

But after years of rolling my eyes at what then felt like a stuffy holier-than-thou platitude, I was forced to reconsider when I hit ultimate burnout. For the majority of my twenties, I had spent my life online and depended on it for my career, but I had started to let it control me. Not comprehending that it was an impossible feat, I tried to structure my life at the pace of the internet, packing my schedule with Twitter friend meet-ups and news events and work obligations and lord knows what else. It didn't even occur to me until it was too late that I didn't really want to be doing any of it, because I was just so *tired*. And all the while, I was refreshing my feeds, trying to figure out how I could be more, more, *more*, not realizing I already was enough, just how I was.

Eventually, I ended up in the hospital with a neurological condition, and I shut down all my social media for six months.

I've since come back online, but as I've worked to improve my self-esteem and adopt a healthier way of living, I've had to learn how to manage my boundaries with social media and my phone so I can use it in a way that *doesn't* make me want to launch myself into a volcano. And here's a shocker for you: it's helped me love myself so, so much more.

If you've picked up this journal, you probably already feel like you should use your phone a little less. But I promise that if you stay with me (and don't abandon the journal for your phone, as tempting as it may be!), you won't just learn how to decrease your screen time—you will stop *wanting* to use your phone, because life around you will seem so much sweeter by comparison.

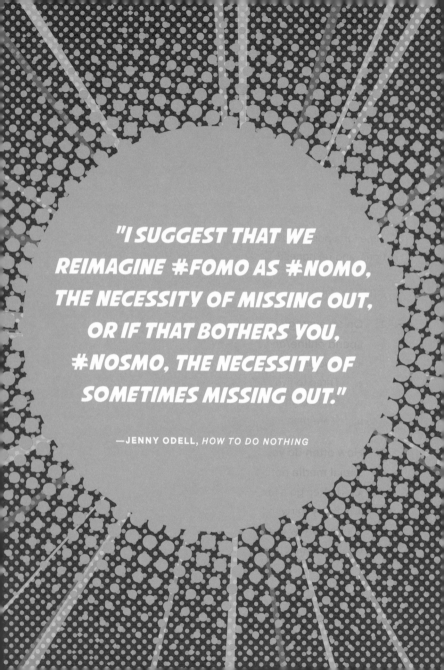

"I SUGGEST THAT WE REIMAGINE #FOMO AS #NOMO, THE NECESSITY OF MISSING OUT, OR IF THAT BOTHERS YOU, #NOSMO, THE NECESSITY OF SOMETIMES MISSING OUT."

—JENNY ODELL, *HOW TO DO NOTHING*

QUIZ:

ARE YOU TOO ONLINE?

Time for a pop quiz. Circle your answers to the following ten questions, and be honest! There's no judgment here.

First, the basics:

1. **On an average day, how many hours do you think you spend online/on your phone?**
    - **A.** Two or less.
    - **B.** Three to five.
    - **C.** Six to eight.
    - **D.** More than eight.

2. **How often do you typically check your phone and/or social media notifications?**
    - **A.** I often go a few hours without checking.
    - **B.** Every thirty minutes to an hour.
    - **C.** Every few minutes.
    - **D.** Pretty much constantly.

3. **Where do you keep your phone at night?**
   A. Charging in another room.
   B. Charging in the bedroom.
   C. On my nightstand.
   D. In the bed, OK?!

4. **When do you first check your phone?**
   A. An hour or more after I've woken up and gotten ready for the day.
   B. Within half an hour.
   C. Within a few minutes.
   D. As soon as I wake up!

5. **In a situation where you're safe but have no cell service or your phone has run out of battery, how do you feel?**
   A. Totally fine—it's no big deal.
   B. A little weird at first, but I adjust!
   C. Stressed—I really want to check my phone.
   D. NO, THANK YOU. Sounds like my nightmare.

6. **Does your phone or social media ever keep you from being fully engaged in other activities or hobbies?**
   A. Never.
   B. Occasionally.
   C. Pretty often, yeah.
   D. Hobbies?

OK, now we're getting real, so buckle up:

7. **How do you tend to feel when you're on social media?**
   - A. Good—I haven't noticed a problem.
   - B. OK, as long as I don't stay on too long.
   - C. FOMO is the primary feeling.
   - D. Like hot garbage, tbh.

8. **Be honest: How often does your phone interrupt quality time with your loved ones or distract you from what they're saying?**
   - A. Never.
   - B. Occasionally.
   - C. Often.
   - D. All the time.

9. **Do you, or does anyone in your life, think you have a problem with your internet use?**
   - A. Nope!
   - B. Maybe . . .
   - C. I could stand to use my phone less.
   - D. Yes, definitely.

THE MOMENT OF TRUTH

Now it's time to total up your answers. For every time you answered A, give yourself one point; for every B, give yourself two points; C, three; and D, four. Total 'em up and see what ya got:

YOU'RE NOT TOO ONLINE (9 TO 14 POINTS)

Why are you even reading this book? Have you read all the books in the world like some fancy book-reading person because you're *sooooo* great, so now you're reading books that don't even apply to you? Disgusting.

YOU'RE A LITTLE TOO ONLINE (15 TO 22 POINTS)

It's nothing extreme, but you could probably stand to be on your phone a little less.

YOU'RE TOO ONLINE (23 TO 31 POINTS)

You're pretty much always on, and the thought of your phone battery going red while you're on the go makes you sweat.

YOU'RE *WAY* TOO ONLINE (32 OR MORE POINTS)

Holy sh*t. Love you, m'dear, but you've got a problem, and you probably already know it. (Don't worry, you're most certainly not alone.)

"I ALWAYS THINK ABOUT THE FACT THAT EVERYTHING REALLY, REALLY AMAZING IN LIFE IS BOTH INEFFICIENT AND ESSENTIALLY BEYOND THE REACH OF TECHNOLOGY. LOVE IS INEFFICIENT, TRUE FRIENDSHIP CAN BE INEFFICIENT, TRUE EXPERIENCE CAN'T BE CAPTURED— I THINK ABOUT TRYING TO SAFE-GUARD THOSE THINGS."

—JIA TOLENTINO

THE REAL,
NO-BULLSH*T PROBLEM
WITH BEING TOO ONLINE

So you've now got some official proof that you're too online. To be fair, who *isn't* these days? It's a bit like driving on the highway—when everyone else on the road is going way over the speed limit, it doesn't seem like a big deal that you're doing it too. (That said, don't do that either, kids.)

After all, what are you *supposed* to do—give up your phone? Disconnect from the modern age? To what end? What will that really change, in the grand scheme of things? No, that's drastic, and also totally unrealistic for most of us who want to maintain our relationships and stay up-to-date on the latest news and/or memes.

Unfortunately, that's exactly how big tech companies are able to reel you in and keep you online, effectively profiting off your attention. And make no mistake, that's precisely what all those social media platforms are vying for: your attention. It's not difficult to break your phone habits because you're weak-willed; tech companies have sunk billions of dollars into making it so. Keeping your eyes on your screen makes them a big ol' pile of cash, after all. Your time is their money, and they have no incentive to respect your autonomy or attention. Their products are addictive by *design*, not because you really like them.

That's not to say you should get off social media entirely. It's not like social media doesn't have its benefits—we're on it for a reason, after all. Rather, it's essential to shift your perspective of your phone not as a fun and innocent little tool, but as another potentially insidious product of capitalism that needs to be *mindfully*, not mindlessly, consumed.

While the concept of getting off social media entirely in today's day and age seems impractical, a reasonable middle ground is not only possible—it's life-changing. And that's with a little thing called *digital minimalism*.

"DIGITAL MINIMALISTS SEE NEW TECHNOLOGIES AS TOOLS TO BE USED TO SUPPORT THINGS THEY DEEPLY VALUE— NOT AS SOURCES OF VALUE THEMSELVES."

—CAL NEWPORT, *DIGITAL MINIMALISM*

DIGITAL DETOXING VS. DIGITAL MINIMALISM: WHAT'S THE DIFFERENCE?

Because capitalism is a menace, there are plenty of companies out there trying to profit off our collective technological burnout by offering luxurious retreats or expensive classes focused on "digital detoxing," which is a fancy way of saying logging the f*ck off for a while (and then inevitably logging back on like nothing happened).

But that's not what we're aiming for. A digital detox is temporary and, on its own, won't lead to any lasting changes. We're not here for that.

Our goal is digital minimalism, or—as computer science professor Cal Newport defines it in his *New York Times*–bestselling book, *Digital Minimalism: Choosing a Focused Life in a Noisy World*—"a philosophy of technology use in which you focus your online time on a small number of carefully selected and optimized activities that strongly support things you value, and then happily miss out on everything else." In other words, it's the Marie Kondo version of using your phone. Making your phone work for *you* instead of the other way around is the key to not losing your actual mind these days.

SETTING THINGS STRAIGHT WHEN THE INTERNET HAS BROKEN YOUR BRAIN

Get specific: *Why* do you want to practice digital minimalism?

....

....

....

....

....

....

....

....

....

....

....

....

....

....

....

....

"AS FAR AS SELF-CONFIDENCE GOES, SO MUCH OF SOCIAL MEDIA IS ABOUT APPROVAL, GETTING LIKES, COMPARING OUR LIVES TO OTHERS'—MEANWHILE, CONFIDENCE IS AN INSIDE JOB, IT'S ABOUT HOW YOU FEEL ABOUT YOURSELF REGARDLESS OF WHAT ANYONE ELSE DOES OR THINKS, IT'S A KNOWING THAT YOU'RE HUMAN, YOU'RE FLAWED, AND YOU'RE AWESOME IN YOUR OWN WAY."

—JEN SINCERO

THE 10 PROMISES OF CUTTING DOWN YOUR SCREEN TIME

[places hand on a picture of Harry Styles] I solemnly swear that practicing digital minimalism—in whatever form works best for you—will lead to:

MORE RESTFUL SLEEP

Unless you've been living under a rock, you've probably heard about all the studies linking late-night screen time with insomnia and disturbed sleep, but it's hard to really believe it until you experience for yourself the effect of unplugging before bed.

SHARPER MEMORY

A lovely effect of paying attention to what's going on around you instead of scrolling.

DECREASED ANXIETY

And FOMO, and all those sh*tty feelings you get when you scroll.
I mean, you'll of course still get bad feelings sometimes, because
that's life, but when you're spending more time focused on your
own life instead of the curated feeds of others, you'll feel a whole
lot lighter.

IMPROVED RELATIONSHIPS
WITH YOUR FRIENDS AND FAMILY

It sounds bizarre, because you probably use your phone to
communicate with them—but less time spent on shallow
communication (liking a friend's post on Instagram) leads to
more time open for actual, real communication (hanging out
with said friend to catch up).

BETTER BOUNDARIES

I don't know about you, but for me, boundaries weren't something I was taught as a kid, and I had to learn the hard way what they were and why I needed them. Developing boundaries around my digital use has helped me extend them to other areas of my life, such as gently saying no to a family member who wanted me to dine at an indoor restaurant during the pandemic. Refusing to let tech companies encroach on my time and attention has encouraged me to apply this same mindfulness in other areas of my life.

MORE TIME

You will be genuinely shocked at how much space you'll free up in your days to do whatever your lovely lil heart desires.

BETTER FOCUS AND PRODUCTIVITY

There's a reason why there are so many apps out there designed specifically to keep you off your phone so you can focus—because it's so easy to let your social media platform of choice destroy your productivity. For me, it's Twitter. Managing my relationship with it has helped me focus on my work when I want to and save social media for breaks and/or downtime.

LIKING THE THINGS YOU DO A HELL OF A LOT MORE

Have you ever been trying to focus on something you usually enjoy doing, only to . . . not really enjoy doing it? I guarantee you that a large portion of this is because the digital attention economy is pulling you this way and that, and you feel fried and exhausted. Digital minimalism will help you actually enjoy what you do.

SAVING MONEY

That's what fewer impulse internet shopping buys will do. Plus, you won't be as focused on what other people have and wear and buy, so you'll be more likely to save your money for what *you* really want.

A BETTER LIFE

I'm not exaggerating here. In today's hyperdigital world, digital minimalism is a major step toward living intentionally in all areas of your life—and living intentionally is, arguably, the only way to truly live your best life.

NOT ALL SOCIAL MEDIA IS BAD!

What platforms might be problem areas for you?

....

....

....

....

....

....

....

....

....

....

YOUR TOP FIVE PLATFORMS, RANKED

Which platforms do you use the most?

- ☐ Twitter
- ☐ Instagram
- ☐ Snapchat
- ☐ TikTok
- ☐ Reddit
- ☐ Other _____
- ☐ Other _____
- ☐ Other _____

Which platforms do you find yourself drawn to for
mindless scrolling?

....

....

....

....

Which platforms do you find yourself drawn to for
deeper connections?

....

....

....

....

What are some things each platform brings to your
life that you struggle to find in real life?

....

....

....

....

....

WHAT ARE YOUR TOP INTERNET STRESSORS?

Go ahead and scroll through social media for the next few minutes (that's right, I'm giving you permission). Pay attention to your body and thoughts, notice what comes up, and take some notes about your responses to the posts you see. No wrong answers here.

In the following pages, write about what gives you joy about social media (e.g., "life updates from friends") and what makes you feel down or anxious (e.g., "posts from exes").

INTERNET STRESSORS

WHAT BRINGS YOU JOY?

....

....

....

....

....

....

....

....

....

....

....

....

....

....

....

....

WHAT MAKES YOU ANXIOUS?

....

....

....

....

....

....

....

....

....

....

....

....

....

....

....

....

CHECK IN

How do your emotions change as you scroll?

....

....

....

....

Is there anything you find yourself hoping to see as you scroll?
Hoping you *don't* see?

....

....

....

....

Scroll through your own social media profiles and consider: what
motivates you to post what you post?

....

....

....

....

....

OK, now let yourself do your own thing on your phone for a while, using it like you would have before you picked up this lovely book. While you do, pay attention to the emotions that come up right before you have an urge to check social media, as well as how you feel afterward. Notice any patterns?

....

....

....

Let's get personal: How do you think your digital use is affecting you? Is there anything in particular you want to change?

....

....

....

What platforms, apps, and/or mediums (e.g., texting) do you think are the biggest problems for you? Why? (Refer back to Not All Social Media Is Bad! on page 20 for a refresher.)

....

....

....

....

....

"I COULD LIVE WITHOUT MY PHONE. . . . I LOVE THE BEACH AND ROCK CLIMBING AND BOXING AND NATURE, SO I LIKE TO STAY AWAY FROM MY PHONE AS MUCH AS POSSIBLE."

—MILLIE BOBBY BROWN

7 (FABULOUSLY SIMPLE) WAYS TO GET STARTED

Getting into new habits is always a little overwhelming, but remember: social media will always be waiting to grab your attention. It's not going anywhere. You, however, can and *will* go many places, because you're a badass. You just gotta take the steps to get there.

Here are a few baby steps you can take right now to experiment with digital minimalism.

TURN OFF PUSH NOTIFICATIONS

This effectively makes your texts and social media like email so that you only check them when you want to. (There are, of course, ways to enable selected push notifications—like from your parents, so they don't get annoyed with you if you don't see their texts.)

EXPRESS YOUR INTENTIONS TO YOUR FRIENDS AND LOVED ONES

Doing this will make you more likely to stick to your intentions so your buds don't roast you for going back on it.

ESTABLISH A CHARGING STATION FOR YOUR PHONE AWAY FROM YOUR BED

(Preferably in another room entirely!)

UNFOLLOW ANY ACCOUNTS THAT MAKE YOU UNHAPPY

You'll probably end up doing this over and over as you become more of a digital minimalist, but doing it at the start is a great way to get yourself thinking about your relationship with social media—and how it alters your IRL relationships.

MAKE A LIST OF HOBBIES AND ACTIVITIES YOU DEEPLY ENJOY

Keep that list handy, and whenever you have an urge to mindlessly check social media or your phone, do one of the things on your list instead. The urge will fade faster than you think, and Future You will be a lot happier with how you spent your time.

DELETE SOCIAL MEDIA APPS FROM YOUR PHONE

This might seem extreme, but it doesn't have to be forever. It's a great strategy if you want to experiment with your relationship with social media without getting rid of it entirely, because hey, you can always check on a computer if you must.

USE TOOLS TO HELP YOU

There are plenty of resources out there to help you on your journey to digital minimalism. Read on to find the right ones for you!

"BREAKING UP WITH YOUR PHONE MEANS GIVING YOURSELF THE SPACE, FREEDOM, AND TOOLS NECESSARY TO CREATE A NEW, LONG-TERM RELATIONSHIP, ONE THAT KEEPS WHAT YOU LOVE ABOUT YOUR PHONE AND GETS RID OF WHAT YOU DON'T."

—CATHERINE PRICE, *HOW TO BREAK UP WITH YOUR PHONE*

BUILDING YOUR
LOGGING-OFF TOOLBOX

Yes, we're about to talk about how you can use apps on your phone to get you off your phone. *Deal with it.* (Just kidding—I'll address that in fun little footnote.*)

Step one is to streamline what you already have. Organize your phone by deleting any apps you rarely or never use and grouping apps by function, which you can then alphabetize or order however makes sense to you.

*Oh, hey there. Now that we're gettin' cozy in this footnote, I'll emphasize that of course, only use these apps if you think they will genuinely help you. You should feel absolutely no pressure to incorporate them into your life if they don't work for you, because that defeats the purpose of digital minimalism!

For example, here are my phone's groups:

ASTROLOGY	**MUSIC**
BROWSERS & SEARCH	**PHONE & SETTINGS**
CALLING & TEXTING	**PHOTO & VIDEO**
DAY PLANNING—e.g., weather apps, calendar apps, Yelp	**SMART DEVICES**—e.g., my cat's automatic feeder app (=^I^=)
DIGITAL MINIMALISM	**SOCIAL MEDIA**—primarily messaging apps
EMAIL	
HEALTH	**TRAVEL**
LEARNING & HOBBIES	**MISCELLANEOUS**—only use this for those annoying undeletable apps no one ever uses
MONEY & SHOPPING	

Once you've organized your phone, it's time to add a few new tools to your belt. Try some of these on for size and see how they work for you.

Forest is the cutest little app that uses the Pomodoro time management method, which breaks up work/study sessions into twenty-five-minute sessions with five-minute breaks between. Sounds painfully boring, right? Well, Forest incentivizes you by letting you "plant" seeds in your forest, and by not using your phone for those twenty-five minutes, you grow a tree. You can grow all different kinds of trees and even team up with a friend. I don't know *why* I find so much joy in planting my little virtual wisteria trees—all I know is that it works.

ForestApp.cc

Freedom works across all your devices to block any distractions (customizable by you) for a set amount of time. You can use it to block yourself from social media during the day except for a set period at night, ensuring that you save your scrolling for a time that *you* control.

Freedom.to

Pocket lets you easily save articles, videos, and stories to check out later. This way, instead of getting your day derailed over and over by content that you probably won't get around to finishing, you can save it to check out all at once at a time of your choosing.

GetPocket.com

For Droid users (represent!), **StayFree** is a screen-time tracker that allows you to limit app usage. It also happens to have the same name as a menstrual pad company, so, ya know, don't get confused.

StayFreeApps.com

IFTTT—which stands for "If This, Then That"—is perfect for creating personalized rules linking together different devices and services, making it ideal for cross-posting across multiple platforms faster and more efficiently, so you can spend less time online.

IFTTT.com

Happy downloading, friend.

TRACK IT

Using your phone's built-in screen-time trackers (like iPhone's Screen Time, Google's Digital Wellbeing, or one of the third-party apps on pages 34–35), start tracking exactly how much you use each group.

WEEK ONE

GROUPS	HOURS/MINUTES
Communication	
Social Media	
Entertainment	
Productivity	
Learning	
Other	
Other	
Other	
TOTAL	

END-OF-WEEK REFLECTION

What went well this week?

....

....

....

....

....

....

....

....

What went poorly this week?

....

....

....

....

....

....

....

....

TRACK IT

Using your phone's built-in screen-time trackers (like iPhone's Screen Time, Google's Digital Wellbeing, or one of the third-party apps on pages 34–35), start tracking exactly how much you use each group.

WEEK TWO

GROUPS	HOURS/MINUTES
Communication	
Social Media	
Entertainment	
Productivity	
Learning	
Other	
Other	
Other	
TOTAL	

END-OF-WEEK REFLECTION

What went well this week?

....

....

....

....

....

....

....

....

What went poorly this week?

....

....

....

....

....

....

....

....

TRACK IT

Using your phone's built-in screen-time trackers (like iPhone's Screen Time, Google's Digital Wellbeing, or one of the third-party apps on pages 34–35), start tracking exactly how much you use each group.

WEEK THREE _____

GROUPS	HOURS/MINUTES
Communication	
Social Media	
Entertainment	
Productivity	
Learning	
Other	
Other	
Other	
TOTAL	

END-OF-WEEK REFLECTION

What went well this week?

....

....

....

....

....

....

....

....

What went poorly this week?

....

....

....

....

....

....

....

....

TRACK IT

Using your phone's built-in screen-time trackers (like iPhone's
Screen Time, Google's Digital Wellbeing, or one of the third-party
apps on pages 34–35), start tracking exactly how much you use
each group.

WEEK FOUR _____

GROUPS	HOURS/MINUTES
Communication	
Social Media	
Entertainment	
Productivity	
Learning	
Other	
Other	
Other	
TOTAL	

END-OF-WEEK REFLECTION

What went well this week?

....

....

....

....

....

....

....

....

What went poorly this week?

....

....

....

....

....

....

....

....

TRACK IT

Using your phone's built-in screen-time trackers (like iPhone's Screen Time, Google's Digital Wellbeing, or one of the third-party apps on pages 34–35), start tracking exactly how much you use each group.

WEEK FIVE

GROUPS	HOURS/MINUTES
Communication	
Social Media	
Entertainment	
Productivity	
Learning	
Other	
Other	
Other	
TOTAL	

END-OF-WEEK REFLECTION

What went well this week?

....

....

....

....

....

....

....

....

What went poorly this week?

....

....

....

....

....

....

....

....

END-OF-MONTH REFLECTION

What goals do you have for next month?

....

....

....

....

....

....

....

....

....

....

....

....

....

....

....

....

....

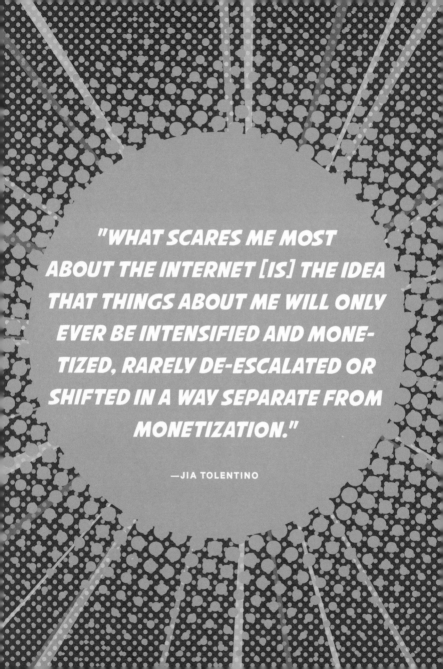

"WHAT SCARES ME MOST ABOUT THE INTERNET [IS] THE IDEA THAT THINGS ABOUT ME WILL ONLY EVER BE INTENSIFIED AND MONETIZED, RARELY DE-ESCALATED OR SHIFTED IN A WAY SEPARATE FROM MONETIZATION."

—JIA TOLENTINO

QUIZ:

WHAT KIND OF DIGITAL MINIMALIZER ARE YOU?

Both in life and in logging off, everyone has a different path. There's no right or wrong way, as long as it feels right to *you*.

That said, knowing your personality and motivations will likely make the transition a little easier. Try taking this quick little quiz to see what kind of digital minimalizer you are.

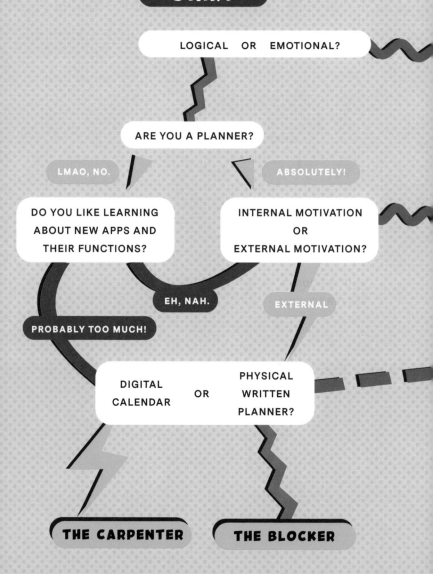

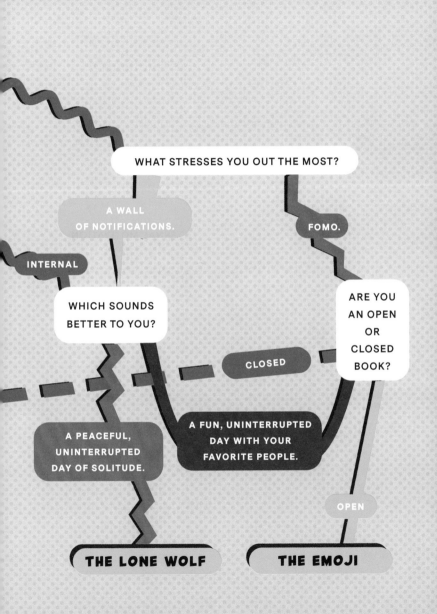

THE CARPENTER

You love learning about new tools at your disposal, and luckily for you, there are a ton out there for digital minimalism. Try out some new apps and strategies (see pages 34–35) that will help you control how you use the internet so you can get the job done.

THE BLOCKER

No, I don't mean blocking people (though hey, you do you). You're the ultimate planner, and blocking out defined segments of your day to answer texts and engage with social media may be the best path for you. (Just don't let yourself get sucked into your screen during the other hours of the day too!)

THE LONE WOLF

All of the digital noise makes you exhausted, and you just want some dang peace and quiet. It'd serve you well to take some alone time, text less, and maybe even get rid of social media for a while as you figure out a healthier relationship with technology. You're an independent bb who needs time alone to shine.

THE EMOJI

You're a people person who uses your feelings as a guide in life, and you should absolutely use them in digital minimalism! Whenever you feel down, think about whether it's a sign to make a change—and not just via temporary action. Don't be shy with the unfollow button, love—and don't forget to enlist your friends for support.

"SO I THINK THAT IT'S IMPORTANT TO NOT PUSH AWAY SOCIAL MEDIA, BECAUSE IT CAN BE REALLY HELPFUL. . . . IT'S LIKE HAVING ONE TAP WITH THE FINGER, MAKING YOU ABLE TO ACTUALLY LEARN ABOUT THE WORLD AND MAYBE FEEL LIKE YOU CAN MAKE A DIFFERENCE AND SUPPORT PEOPLE THAT YOU LOVE AND FIGHT FOR OTHER PEOPLE AND FIGHT FOR YOURSELF."

—BILLIE EILISH

HOW TO USE SOCIAL MEDIA WITHOUT FEELING LIKE SH*T

OK, hear me out. I propose one simple rule that, if you get yourself in the habit of following it, will keep you from feeling, well, like sh*t: *Pay attention to how you feel when you're on social media, and when you notice that you're feeling bad, log off.*

That's all. It sounds kind of annoying, I know, but it really is that simple. The trouble is, it doesn't *seem* that simple before you've a) used your time off social media to do things you enjoy that make you think, "I'd rather be doing this than watching so-and-so's Instagram Story that always makes me feel like sh*t about myself"; and b) learned to genuinely notice *and respect* how you feel. You can't notice that you're feeling bad if you're numb to your emotions, and you can't address that you're feeling bad if you shame yourself for feeling bad.

But unfortunately, us human beings tend to tense up against bad feelings by trying to convince ourselves we're not really feeling them, and it stops us from taking steps to address those feelings, like logging off and doing something kind for ourselves. Instead, we keep watching that Instagram Story that makes us feel like hot garbage, and we feel worse, so we keep watching Instagram Stories, hoping that something will pop up that somehow makes us feel better, but obviously that doesn't happen, so we feel even worse . . . rinse and repeat. Fun stuff!

These shame spirals are also excellent for social media companies because they keep you online, feeling bad about yourself and maybe occasionally clicking on a sneakily advertised product exploiting your deepest insecurities, which these companies have gleaned via extensive data mining.

But if you log off, telling yourself that you're allowed to have these feelings and thinking about why they might have come up, you may figure out a concrete action step—like unfollowing that Instagram account that keeps bringing you down or ditching that friend that always seems to *purposely* post things to make you feel FOMO—that will likely lead to real life satisfaction.

So I implore you: Pay attention to how you feel. *Respect* how you feel. Your feelings are here to tell you something, if you give them the time, space, and dignity to speak to you.

And when you're on social media and you notice that you're feeling bad? Log off. You owe it to yourself, bb.

TRACK IT

Color in or circle how you felt while using social media every day this month.

MONTH _____

DAY 1 _____   ☹️ 😐 🙂 😃

DAY 2 _____   ☹️ 😐 🙂 😃

DAY 3 _____   ☹️ 😐 🙂 😃

DAY 4 _____   ☹️ 😐 🙂 😃

DAY 5 _____   ☹️ 😐 🙂 😃

Notes:

....

....

....

....

TRACK IT

DAY 6
_____

☹ 😐 🙂 😃

DAY 7
_____

☹ 😐 🙂 😃

DAY 8
_____

☹ 😐 🙂 😃

DAY 9
_____

☹ 😐 🙂 😃

DAY 10
_____

☹ 😐 🙂 😃

Notes:

....

....

....

....

....

....

....

TRACK IT

DAY 11
_____ ☹ 😐 🙂 😃

DAY 12
_____ ☹ 😐 🙂 😃

DAY 13
_____ ☹ 😐 🙂 😃

DAY 14
_____ ☹ 😐 🙂 😃

DAY 15
_____ ☹ 😐 🙂 😃

Notes:

....

....

....

....

....

....

....

TRACK IT

DAY 16
_____

☹ 😐 🙂 😃

DAY 17
_____

☹ 😐 🙂 😃

DAY 18
_____

☹ 😐 🙂 😃

DAY 19
_____

☹ 😐 🙂 😃

DAY 20
_____

☹ 😐 🙂 😃

Notes:

....

....

....

....

....

....

....

TRACK IT

DAY 21

_____

😦 😐 🙂 😄

DAY 22

_____

😦 😐 🙂 😄

DAY 23

_____

😦 😐 🙂 😄

DAY 24

_____

😦 😐 🙂 😄

DAY 25

_____

😦 😐 🙂 😄

Notes:

....

....

....

....

....

....

....

TRACK IT

DAY 26
_____ 🙁 😐 🙂 😃

DAY 27
_____ 🙁 😐 🙂 😃

DAY 28
_____ 🙁 😐 🙂 😃

DAY 29
_____ 🙁 😐 🙂 😃

DAY 30
_____ 🙁 😐 🙂 😃

DAY 31
_____ 🙁 😐 🙂 😃

Notes:

....

....

....

....

....

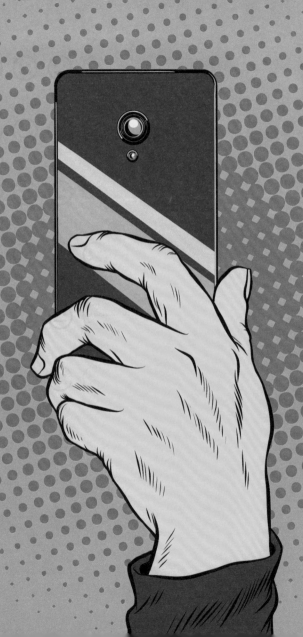

END-OF-MONTH REFLECTION

WHAT IRL ACTIVITIES DID YOU PARTICIPATE IN?

....

....

....

....

....

....

....

....

....

....

....

....

....

....

....

....

....

....

HOW DID YOU FEEL BEFORE, DURING, OR AFTER?

"REVENGE BEDTIME PROCRASTINATION (RBP) [IS] A TERM THAT DESCRIBES WHEN PEOPLE WHO DON'T HAVE MUCH CONTROL OVER THEIR DAYTIME LIFE CATEGORICALLY REFUSE TO GO TO BED EARLY IN ORDER TO REGAIN SOME SENSE OF FREEDOM DURING THE LATE-NIGHT HOURS."

—ALESSANDRA EDWARDS

HOW TO STOP YOUR PHONE FROM INTERRUPTING YOUR SHUT-EYE

How many times have you found yourself scrolling on your phone at 1 a.m.? (No judgment here, because for me, the answer is "I don't want to know.")

Those big tech companies don't care about your beauty sleep. In fact, they'd much rather you be online than taking care of yourself. They *want* you to take your phone into bed with you so they can try to get your attention every hour of the day—even though studies have shown the blue light from screens causes sleep disruptions.

It sucks, but it's up to you to preserve your evenings so you can get restful, uninterrupted, screenless time to unwind before bed and sleep through the night. Here are a few tips to stop your phone from interrupting your shut-eye.

SERIOUSLY, GET IT THE HELL OUT OF YOUR BEDROOM

If you *must* keep your phone in your bedroom, turn it off every night until morning, at least half an hour before you go to bed. I know, it sucks, but this is a biggie.

BUY A REAL ALARM CLOCK

Or use anything that's not your phone (I use my Google Home). That way, you can't get around my first point by being all BuT mY pHoNe Is My aLaRm ClOcK. Sorry, my sweet little tater tot.

FIND A RELAXING ACTIVITY TO DO BEFORE BED

Reading, crafting, taking a soothing bath . . . do literally anything that gives you joy and peace, as long as it doesn't involve a screen. Try to make time to do it for at least half an hour before you wind down for bed—and *after* you've set your devices aside for the night. This will give you real, deep-seated motivation to slow down your brain before you ~power down.~ (Get it? Because phones.)

KEEP A BOOK, PUZZLE, OR OTHER SCREENLESS ACTIVITY NEXT TO YOUR BED

This is in case you can't sleep, so you have less of an urge to get up and get your phone, which *should not be in your bedroom.* I'm saying it a third time in case three is the magic number, to get it into your wonderful, glorious brain.

"I LOVE MY JOURNAL AS MUCH AS I LOVE MY PHONE. I FIND IT TO BE A BIG PART OF MY SELF-CARE TO REFLECT ON MY DAY AND WRITE WORDS THAT INSPIRE ME OR PASTE BUSINESS CARDS AND PICTURES."

—FRANCHESCA RAMSEY

THE 14-DAY CHALLENGE

OK, enough with the talk: It's time to get real. Ready? Here we go.

The following is a two-week plan for rolling back your social media use and embracing digital minimalism. During week one, you'll be giving up* any and all optional screen time. This is important because a week later, you'll be able to slowly reintegrate tech back into your life with a clear head, like a true digital minimalist: only using tech in a way that strongly supports the things you value, so you can miss out on the rest with no regrets.

This means that if you mess up and give in to a social media urge in the first week, you have to start all over from the beginning. I'm harsh because I love you, babe.

During week two, you are allowed to reintegrate one service, app, or platform a day, but your total recreational screen time can't exceed one hour. For example: you might decide to reintegrate TikTok on Day 8, Twitter on Day 9, and Snapchat on Day 10, so on Day 10, you're allowed to use any combination of TikTok, Twitter, or Snapchat for one hour *total*.

*Oh, hi there. Just want to highlight that of course, exceptions exist—for example: if you need to use your phone or social media for your job, or you depend on text alerts from your family, or anything else that is of genuinely high importance. Privilege is real, and those with less of it may not be able to take on this challenge as literally. That's OK and doesn't mean digital minimalism isn't for you. As long as you trust and stay honest with yourself, you can take on this challenge in any form you need. Know that there is no wrong way—there are only ways that feel right and wrong to *you.*

This time restriction will help you see a) which platforms brings actual value to your life vs. which ones merely take time; b) how you actually spend time using social media; and c) what you're really missing out on when you're not online (spoiler: nothing). You may also find that you'll miss a lot fewer platforms than you'd think.

What you'll need: a pen and a sheet of small stickers that make you happy whenever you look at them.

WEEK ONE: GOIN' COLD TURKEY

Keep any daily observations here. Was today harder? Easier?
What did you spend your time on? How are your emotions
changing? Are you craving social media? Remember: there's
no "right" way to feel!

☐ **DAY 1** *Give yourself a sticker in the box for every day
you don't use screens recreationally!*

....

....

....

....

....

....

....

....

....

....

....

....

....

☐ **DAY 2**

....

....

....

....

....

....

....

....

☐ **DAY 3**

....

....

....

....

....

....

....

....

☐ **DAY 4**

....

....

....

....

....

....

....

....

☐ **DAY 5**

....

....

....

....

....

....

....

....

☐ **DAY 6**

....
....
....
....
....
....
....
....

☐ **DAY 7**

....
....
....
....
....
....
....
....

WEEK TWO: REINTEGRATION

☐ **DAY 8**

....
....
....
....
....
....
....
....
....
....
....
....
....
....
....
....

☐ **DAY 9**

....

....

....

....

....

....

....

☐ **DAY 10**

....

....

....

....

....

....

....

☐ **DAY 11**

....

....

....

....

....

....

....

☐ **DAY 12**

....

....

....

....

....

....

....

☐ **DAY 13**

☐ **DAY 14**

END-OF-CHALLENGE REFLECTION

WHAT IRL ACTIVITIES DID YOU PARTICIPATE IN?

HOW DID YOU FEEL BEFORE, DURING, OR AFTER?

"WE LIVE IN A TECHNOLOGICAL UNIVERSE IN WHICH WE ARE ALWAYS COMMUNICATING. AND YET WE HAVE SACRIFICED CONVERSATION FOR MERE CONNECTION."

—SHERRY TURKLE

THE ANATOMY OF GOOD LISTENING

At first, the concept of a phone-free conversation might feel a little daunting. Granted, there is something comforting about knowing your phone is there to fill awkward silences if you need it. But humans are social creatures, and your body knows how to listen intentionally—if your mind will let it.

Read on for a few pointers on how to be a good listener.

1. Mind: Do your best to notice when your mind is wandering and, instead of panicking or scolding yourself, gently bring it back to the present moment.

2. Eyes: Look at the person you're speaking with, not your screen! If you have a hard time with eye contact, it's OK—looking at their hands is a neutral place that will still help you stay on track.

3. Ears: If you're having a hard time focusing on what your friend is saying, take a second to really appreciate the sound of their voice. It will help remind you why you *want* to be listening to them.

4. Lungs: If you feel yourself getting anxious and feel the familiar pull to grab your phone, take a deep breath and exhale slowly. Exhaling longer than you inhale sends a signal to your brain to relax. (Try it a few times now—it really does work!)

5. Arms: It may seem silly, but trust me: it's a lot easier to pay attention when you're feeling comfortable and cozy. When you're spending intentional time with friends, wear things that make you feel comfortable and confident so you can be focused on what they're saying instead of how *cold* it is right now, or how the shirt you're wearing feels a little too tight in the armpits.

6. Hands: If you really need to do something with your hands, there's no shame! Buy yourself a fidget spinner or another stimulation toy that you can absentmindedly fiddle with while you listen.

7. Legs: Feel too restless for a seated one-on-one? Suggest to your companion that you walk and talk instead. The movement and fresh air will help you focus on what they're saying instead of your fidgety legs or your phone in your pocket.

ACTIVE LISTENING

Talking to strangers (scary, I know!) has been shown to improve mood and self-esteem and provide a greater sense of well-being. Write down some conversations you've had with strangers that would not have happened otherwise. Reflect on how you felt afterward.

....

....

....

....

....

....

....

....

....

....

....

....

....

....

....

"ACCORDING TO STUDIES CONDUCTED BY THE JOURNAL OF ENVIRONMENTAL SCIENCE AND TECHNOLOGY, GETTING OUTSIDE FOR AS LITTLE AS FIVE MINUTES AT A TIME IMPROVES MOOD AND SELF-ESTEEM. SO WHAT ARE WE DOING? THERE'S A WHOLE WORLD OUT THERE! THERE ARE BEACHES TO DRINK MARGS ON, BIRDS TO HEAR CHIRPING, BUTTERFLIES TO CHASE, TRAILS TO HIKE, POOL PARTIES TO BE HAD."

—MELEAH BOWLES, *LIFE UNPLUGGED*

SO WHAT ARE YOU GONNA DO INSTEAD?

Digital detoxes are unsustainable. We live in a digital world, and you're a super cool person with things to do. But I hope this experience will show you that a different relationship with technology is not only possible—it will reap the rewards your awesome lil self deserves.

Social media companies don't deserve your time—you do. If you want to give 'em a little bit of it, go for it—but even still, you'll find that you have tons of newfound free time at your disposal, as long as you practice digital minimalism.

So . . . whatcha gonna do?

ACTIVITIES YOU CAN DO INSTEAD

- Go somewhere in nature and listen for three minutes. Record what you heard.

- Go for a phoneless walk and see if you spot anything you've never noticed before.

- Open a cookbook you have (or get one from the library) and make a brand-new recipe.

- Think about a creative project you've always wanted to start. Why not start it now?

Make a list of three things you've done this week that made you feel energized. What were they?

1.

....

....

....

2.

....

....

....

3.

....

....

....

Make a list of three things you've done this week that made you feel drained. What were they?

1.

....

....

....

2.

....

....

....

3.

....

....

....

INTENTIONAL TIME

List the person or people you communicate with most in your life. What is meaningful to you about your relationship(s)? In what ways are you connected and what role do you play in maintaining that connection?

....

....

....

....

....

....

....

....

....

....

....

....

....

....

....

....

List five people you'd like to connect with more.

1.

....

....

2.

....

....

3.

....

....

4.

....

....

5.

....

....

List five places you'd like to visit.

1.

....

....

2.

....

....

3.

....

....

4.

....

....

5.

....

....

List five hobbies you'd like to explore.

1.

....

....

2.

....

....

3.

....

....

4.

....

....

5.

....

....

WHAT WILL YOUR FUTURE LOOK LIKE?

What makes you happy? (There are no wrong answers!)

....

....

....

....

....

....

....

....

....

....

....

....

....

....

....

....

....

....

How can you bring more of what makes you happy into your life?

....

....

....

....

....

....

....

....

....

....

....

....

....

....

....

....

....

What are three screenless goals for yourself this year?

1.

....

....

....

2.

....

....

....

3.

....

....

....

How can you take action toward those goals this month?

....

....

....

....

....

....

....

....

....

....

....

....

....

....

....

....

....

....

This week?

....

....

....

....

....

....

....

....

Today?

....

....

....

....

....

....

....

....

....

Has your perspective changed since you started your digital
minimalism journey? How?

....

....

....

....

....

....

....

....

....

....

....

....

....

....

....

....

....

....

Social media companies want you to spend your whole life on your phone. How do *you* want to spend your life?

....

....

....

....

....

....

....

....

....

....

....

....

....

....

....

....

....

....

NOTES

ACKNOWLEDGMENTS

First of all, thank you to my wonderful agent, Dana Murphy, without whom I would have pulled out every last hair on my head, and to my brilliant editor, Jill Saginario, without whom this book would not exist.

I also must thank my best friend and cheerleader, Kayla, for reminding me that I *can* write a book and also that I'm a living, breathing human who needs to rest sometimes; my therapist, Jenn, for gently reminding me to log off social media *well before* this book was in the works; and Diet Coke, for always being there for me.

ABOUT THE AUTHOR

SAMMY NICKALLS is a freelance writer for *Teen Vogue* and former editor at *Adweek* and *Esquire*. Sammy created the hashtag #TalkingAboutIt, which invites social media users to share about their mental health openly and honestly. She is currently pursuing her master's degree in clinical mental health counseling.

Printed in China

SPRUCE BOOKS with colophon is a registered trademark
of Penguin Random House LLC

26 25 24 23 22   9 8 7 6 5 4 3 2 1

Text: Sammy Nickalls
Illustrations © Valeriy Kachaev | Dreamstime.com
Editor: Jill Saginario
Production editor: Bridget Sweet
Designer: Alicia Terry

ISBN: 978-1-63217-411-6

Sasquatch Books
1904 Third Avenue, Suite 710
Seattle, WA 98101

SasquatchBooks.com